D1256108

Date _____

Dear _____

_____

_____

_____

_____

_____

_____

From

_____

May God Comfort You

© 2005 by Roy Lessin

© 2005 Christian Art Gifts, RSA
        Christian Art Gifts Inc., IL, USA

Designed by Christian Art Gifts

Scripture taken from the *Holy Bible*, King James Version.
Copyright © 1962 by The Zondervan Corporation. Used by permission.

Printed in China

ISBN 1-86920-335-6

05 06 07 08 09 10 11 12 13 14 – 10 9 8 7 6 5 4 3 2 1

May God Comfort You

Roy Lessin

christian
art gifts

Contents

"Blessed be God, even the
Father of our Lord Jesus Christ,
the Father of mercies, and the
God of all comfort; who comforteth
us in all our tribulation, that we
may be able to comfort them
which are in any trouble,
by the comfort wherewith we
ourselves are comforted of God."

- 2 Corinthians 1:3-4

God of all Comfort

The God of all comfort

God is the God of all comfort. He has
all the comfort you need for all the
circumstances of life that you will ever
walk through. He is not just the God
of all comfort at the graveside, but He is
also the God of all comfort in life's trials,
tests, difficulties, and hardships. He is
the God of all comfort in the valleys, the
desert places, the lonely places, the
silent places, and the dark places of life.
He comforts you with hope, truth,
light, and most of all His presence.

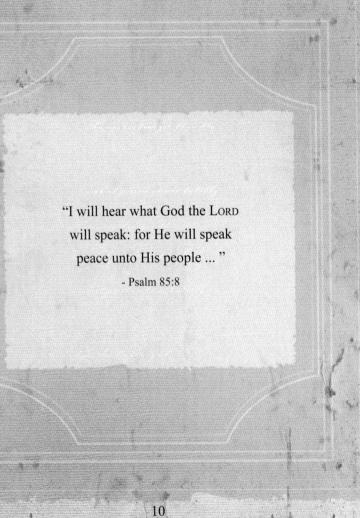

"I will hear what God the Lord
will speak: for He will speak
peace unto His people ... "

- Psalm 85:8

A voice like none other

When God comforts you He speaks to you with a voice like none other. It is a voice of peace and calm assurance.

It is not an upbraiding, demanding, condemning, or berating voice. His voice does not say, "go away," but rather, "come close."

God's voice is a voice with the sound of healing in every syllable, a voice with the sound of strength in every word, and a voice with the sound of consolation in every sentence.

His voice soothes your soul and calms your fears; it nourishes your life and quiets your thoughts; it builds your spirit and warms your heart.

"The eternal God is thy
refuge, and underneath
are the everlasting arms."

- Deuteronomy 33:27

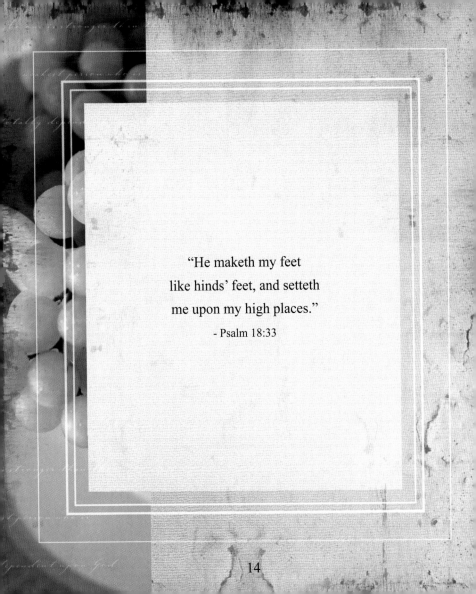

"He maketh my feet
like hinds' feet, and setteth
me upon my high places."

- Psalm 18:33

Safe in His strength

When God comforts you His arms draw you close. He bathes you in His peace, covers you with His grace, and wraps you in His love. In His arms you know that you are shielded; in His presence you know that you have courage; in His strength you know that you are safe.

His arms lift you above everything that tries to pull you down, they shield you from everything that tries to come against you, and they carry you through everything that tries to pull you back.

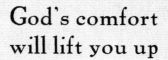

God's comfort will lift you up

God's comfort *goes deeper than any*
valley you walk through *and* it
will lift you higher than any mountain
that you face. It is a penetrating
comfort that touches you at
the deepest level of who you are.

A peaceful haven

When your soul is in turmoil upon the troubled sea of life, God's comfort brings you to a peaceful haven.

When your heart is heavy with a great burden, His comfort releases you and lightens your load.

When your spirit is troubled because of something that has brought pain, His comfort is a healing balm that refreshes and restores you.

"That by two immutable things,
in which it was impossible for God
to lie, we might have a strong consolation,
who have fled for refuge to lay hold
upon the hope set before us:
Which hope we have as an anchor
of the soul, both sure and stedfast."

- Hebrews 6:18-19

God of all Comfort

Courage to move on

God's comfort is filled with hope.
God never puts you down or pulls you down.
He is the God of the future and
the God of all your tomorrows.
He has a plan and purpose for your life,
and His comfort assures you of His power
to fulfill all that is in His heart for you.

His comfort causes your eyes to see
far enough ahead so that you can take
the next step in your journey with the confidence
of faith. His comfort moves you beyond the
temporal into the eternal things that He is
preparing for you. His comfort gives you the
courage to move on, press on, fight on, and
keep on with sure resolve that all will be well.

Never comfortless

"I will not leave you
comfortless: I will come to you."

- John 14:18

God's comfort will not fail or falter.

He will never lead you somewhere and then abandon you; He will never assure you of His presence and then desert you; He will never call you to His presence and then turn aside.

His comfort will always be there at the perfect moment, even in the midst of the most difficult circumstances.

The certainty
of His comfort

His comfort is as:

- certain as His word,
- reliable as His character,
- assuring as His love,
- affirming as His goodness,
- abundant as His grace,
- complete as His mercies, and
- dependable as His faithfulness.

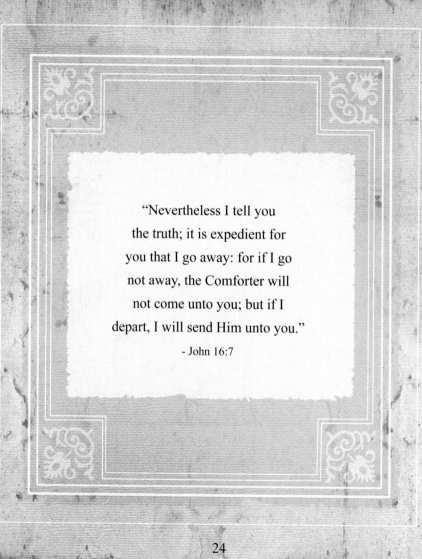

"Nevertheless I tell you
the truth; it is expedient for
you that I go away: for if I go
not away, the Comforter will
not come unto you; but if I
depart, I will send Him unto you."

- John 16:7

The Comforter

"I will pray the Father, and He
shall give you another Comforter,
that He may abide with you for ever."

- John 14:16

When it came time for Jesus to leave this earth
He did not want to leave you alone. He knew
what you would face and what you needed.

In His love for you, He knew that He could
not give you anything less than Himself. He
could only send you someone who could be
the perfect provision, not a partial solution, to
all the things you would walk through in life.
Because of this, He called the One who would
come to you, "The Comforter".

The Holy Spirit is called the Comforter because of who He is in His nature, and what He does through His actions.

He hasn't come to give you theories about how you should live, or to tell you to work things out in your own way. He has come because He knows that you cannot work things out on your own.

The Holy Spirit is called the Comforter because He comes to you, not for the momentary need, but for the long haul.

He is the Comforter because He is with you, beside you, around you, and within you. He is the Comforter because He brings to you the Father's love.

One of the main ministries of the Holy Spirit is to give you comfort by being your comfort.

One important way that He does this is by speaking the truth to you. Lies, deceptions, half-truths, exaggerations, and false hopes do not bring true comfort.

The Comforter doesn't comfort you by pretending that what you are going through isn't real. He doesn't comfort you with fantasy, but with reality.

He comforts you by telling you that Jesus loves you, that your Heavenly Father cares for you, that God has a purpose for you, that a place in heaven is being prepared for you, that Jesus is coming for you, and that, although many things are hard now, they cannot be compared to the things that God has waiting for you.

"But when the Comforter is come,
whom I will send unto you
from the Father, even the Spirit of
truth, which proceedeth from
the Father, He shall testify of Me."

- John 15:26

"For as the sufferings of Christ abound in us, so our consolation also aboundeth by Christ. And whether we be afflicted, it is for your consolation and salvation, which is effectual in the enduring of the same sufferings which we also suffer: or whether we be comforted, it is for your consolation and salvation. And our hope of you is stedfast, knowing, that as ye are partakers of the sufferings, so shall ye be also of the consolation."

- 2 Corinthians 1:5-7

God of all Comfort

God's great consolation

God's comfort means consolation. It is a beautiful word that draws you to the place of refuge from the storm, deliverance from the battle, shade from the heat, soothing from the pain, and shelter from every peril.

God doesn't measure out consolation through an eye-drop, but with an abounding measure. Whatever the intensity of your difficulty may be, His consolation is not equal to it, but greater than it.

Consolation eases the pressure, reduces the intensity, and lightens the load of every test of faith. Consolation says to every storm of life, "You may go this far, but no further."

"Now our Lord Jesus Christ
Himself, and God, even our Father,
which hath loved us, and hath
given us everlasting consolation
and good hope through grace,
comfort your hearts, and stablish
you in every good word and work."

- 2 Thessalonians 2:16-17

The comfort of compassion

When a child hurts himself
he runs to his mother's arms for comfort.
What is it that a child finds
when he is in his mother's arms?
Why does he go to her and not another?
Is it not because the mother's love draws him,
the mother's arms assure him,
the mother's touch soothes him,
the mother's voice quiets him,
and the mother's heart responds to him
with all the compassion that is within her!

"To appoint unto them that mourn
in Zion, to give unto them beauty
for ashes, the oil of joy for
mourning, the garment of praise
for the spirit of heaviness; that
they might be called trees of
righteousness, the planting
of the LORD, that He might be glorified."

- Isaiah 61:3

Relief, release and rest

Every person of the triune Godhead – Father, Son, and Holy Spirit – responds to you in your time of need. They are all involved in the ministry of your consolation and comfort.

When you are hurting they are present to bring you relief, release, and rest. All that is needed is for you to open your heart and receive the comfort they so desire to give.

It grieves the heart of God when His people do not respond to His call, pull away from His arms, or do not come under the covering He extends to them. *"O Jerusalem, Jerusalem ... how often would*

I have gathered thy children together, as a hen doth gather her brood under her wings, and ye would not!" (Lk. 13:34). He loves you so much and it gladdens His heart to know that you seek His comfort.

God also comforts you so that He can comfort others through you. God uses the comforted as comforters.

When God leads you through a dark valley, you can lead others to His footsteps; when He brings you out of the darkness, you can point others to His light; when He soothes your pain, you can carry others to His healing touch.

"And whether we be afflicted,
it is for your consolation and
salvation, which is effectual
in the enduring of the same
sufferings which we also suffer:
or whether we be comforted, it is
for your consolation and salvation."

- 2 Corinthians 1:6

"Father, whate'er of earthly bliss
Thy sovereign will denies;
Accepted at the throne of grace
let this petition rise;
Give me a calm and thankful heart
from every murmur free,
The blessing of Thy grace impart
and let me live to Thee."
- Anne Steele

"Abide with me – fast falls the eventide;

The darkness deepens – Lord, with me abide!

When other helpers fail and comforts flee,

Help of the helpless, oh, abide with me!"

- Henry F. Lyte

Every winter will be followed by spring

As God comforts us He reminds us that every night season knows the dawn; that every winter is followed by spring; that every storm is followed by calm.

His comfort brings hope instead of hopelessness, and rest instead of despair. He is the One who is the lifter of your head, the guardian of your pathway, and the companion who stays closer than a brother.

"But Thou, O Lord, art a shield
for me; my glory, and the lifter up
of mine head. I cried unto the Lord
with my voice, and He heard me out
of His holy hill. Selah. I laid me
down and slept; I awaked;
for the Lord sustained me."

- Psalm 3:3-5

God's comfort

Through God's comfort He will keep you from giving up or giving in to anything that tries to move you away from His purpose for your life. He is the One who will put a song in your heart again.

"The Spirit of the Lord is upon me,
because He hath anointed me to
preach the gospel to the poor; He
hath sent me to heal the brokenhearted,
to preach deliverance to the captives,
and recovering of sight to the blind,
to set at liberty them that are bruised."

- Luke 4:18

He will never fail you

Through faith, God wants you to fall back into His arms of love. He wants you to lean upon Him with all your heart and all your trust. He will not fail you, forsake you, or let you down. He is your Heavenly Father, and He is your God of all comfort.

"Comfort ye, comfort ye

My people, saith your God."

- Isaiah 40:1